THE ABIDING CONTRACTOR

TRACKING INSURANCE, ELIMINATING RISK, AND AVOIDING CATASTROPHE

DOUG GROVES

Internet addresses given in this book were accurate at the time it went to press.

Printed in the United States of America

Published in Hellertown, PA

Cover design by Leanne Coppola

Library of Congress Control Number 2026904695

ISBN 979-8-89420-090-3

For more information or to place bulk orders, contact the author or the publisher at Jennifer@BrightCommunications.net.

CONTENTS

INTRODUCTION

Builders and general contractors rely on many subcontractors to complete projects safely, on time, and within budget. Yet insurance compliance between contractors and subcontractors is often handled informally—"on good faith"—which creates significant exposure.

This mini-book condenses core lessons from my book *The Abiding Franchisor* and adapts them for the construction world. It includes information on why insurance compliance matters to builders and contractors, what insurances to require of your subcontractors, how to track those insurances efficiently and effectively, and a practical five-step system to reduce your risk.

WHY INSURANCE COMPLIANCE MATTERS

Compliance with insurance rules and regulations is just as important for builders and contractors as it is for any other professional. Here's why.

- Legal and financial protection: Proper insurance for each trade protects the general contractor, owner, and subcontractors from liability, property loss, and claims costs.
- Contractual obligation: Your construction contracts typically require subcontractors to carry specified coverages and limits, and to name the contractor and owner as additional insured.
- Ensuring successful risk transfer: Risk transfer only works when insurance compliance is correctly documented. Certificates of insurance (COIs) and policy endorsements prove compliance. Without documentation, you might be left defending claims or paying losses.

- Volume and variability: One project might have dozens of subcontractors, and it might be possible to track their insurance compliance. However, across many projects, tracking hundreds of policies annually becomes overwhelming—unless you have a system.

COMMON GAPS AND PITFALLS

From my decades of experience in the insurance industry working with contractors and other business owners, I've seen well-meaning people fall into these common gaps and pitfalls.

- Relying on verbal assurances that their subcontractors have the required insurance.
- Receiving nonstandard Certificates of Insurance (COIs) or incomplete paperwork.
- Being unaware that subcontractors have missed their insurance expiration dates and not submitted their renewal certificates.
- Not realizing that their subcontractors purchased insurance with insufficient limits—or even the wrong insurance coverage types entirely.
- Not checking that they were named as additional insured on their subcontractors' insurance policies, or missing the right endorsement language.
- Lacking a centralized system for tracking their subcontractors' insurance.
- Permitting different subs to submit proof of their insurance in different formats.

KEY INSURANCE COVERAGES TO REQUIRE

As a builder or contractor, you are likely to hire many subcontractors who perform different trades for different projects. This list shows the key insurances you should require—by trade and project type.

- General Liability Insurance (primary insurance): This protects against claims for bodily injury and property damage to third parties. It is essential for all subcontractors.
- Commercial Auto Liability: This is required when subs use vehicles for a job.
- Workers' Compensation: State-mandated for employees, this insurance is critical to avoid exposure in cases of jobsite injuries.
- Professional Liability (where applicable): For trades with design or technical services, such as engineers and surveyors, this is key.
- Umbrella/Excess Liability: This type of insurance provides higher limits than primary policies, which makes it useful for high-exposure projects.

- Builder's Risk (usually required by owner): For property damage to work-in-progress; often procured by owner or GC.
- Pollution/Environmental (if applicable): For trades handling hazardous materials.

CONTRACT LANGUAGE ESSENTIALS

To protect your company, be sure to include these details in your contracts with your subcontractors.

- Required coverages and minimum limits: State minimums are rarely sufficient, so specify project-appropriate limits.
- Named additional insureds: List the general contractor and owner of the subcontractor's company (and insurers' required wording).
- Primary and noncontributory clause: The subcontractor's policy should be the primary one, and it should not seek contribution from the general contractor's/owner's insurance.
- Waiver of subrogation in favor of the general contractor/owner where appropriate.
- Requirements for when subcontractors must send you their certificates of insurance (COIs) certificates and endorsements, including what the COIs must show and which endorsements must be attached.
- Timelines: These include how long before mobilization COIs must be received and how many days

before expiration must insurance renewals be processed.

- Remedies for noncompliance: These consequences might include withholding the subcontractor's payments, removal from the worksite, and termination of the subcontractor's rights.

PRACTICAL CERTIFICATE TRACKING: WHY YOU NEED A SYSTEM

Manually reviewing certificates of insurance (COIs) is slow, and it's easy to miss details and make errors. However, an experienced insurance professional can read and validate certificates quickly. Standardization and automation reduce errors, save time, and ensure continuous insurance compliance.

INTRODUCING AN ADAPTED "EZCERT" FOR CONTRACTORS

You can implement a certificate-tracking program that's tailored to builders and contractors. Its core features include the following.

- Centralized repository for COIs and endorsements
- Standard submission format and checklist for subs
- Automated alerts for upcoming expirations and missing documentation
- Trained staff or service to validate coverage types, limits, additional insured wording, and primary/noncontributory language
- Monthly compliance reports by project and subcontractor

THE FIVE-STEP PROCESS FOR ROBUST INSURANCE COMPLIANCE

It's this simple!

STEP 1: DEFINE REQUIREMENTS UPFRONT

- In contract documents and bid packages, clearly state required coverages, limits, additional insured language, and submission deadlines.
- Use checklists on bid forms to ensure potential subs understand requirements before award.

STEP 2: STANDARDIZE SUBMISSION

- Provide a standard COI template and a simple submission portal or email format.
- Require that specific endorsements (additional insured, primary/noncontributory, waiver of subrogation) be uploaded along with the COI.

STEP 3: VERIFY AND VALIDATE

Have trained personnel (an internal risk manager or outsourced service) review each COI and endorsements for:

- Correct coverage types and adequate limits
- Proper naming of additional insureds and correct endorsement forms
- Effective dates that cover the project duration and include renewals
- Primary/noncontributory and waiver language as required

STEP 4: TRACK RENEWALS AND EXPIRATIONS

- Use software or a service that flags upcoming expirations at multiple intervals (60/30/14/7 days) and notifies subs and the general contractor.
- Do not allow continuation of work without proof of renewal. Enforce contract remedies for noncompliance.

STEP 5: REPORT AND ENFORCE

- Produce regular compliance reports for each project, listing compliant and noncompliant subs.
- Enforce contractual actions consistently: Stop work, withhold payment, or replace subcontractors who fail to comply.
- Maintain records as proof of diligence; these records are crucial if a claim or litigation arises.

CHECKLIST FOR ONBOARDING AND ONGOING MANAGEMENT

- Before mobilization: receive COI and required endorsements showing the general contractor/owner as additional insured.
- Confirm workers' compensation coverage for subs with employees.
- Confirm commercial auto insurance for subs using vehicles on the project.
- Confirm that policy dates cover the whole period of exposure.
- Confirm that the limits meet contract requirements; verify that an umbrella/excess policy applies to underlying policies.
- Ensure proper endorsement wording (sample wording saved in contract docs).
- Set reminders for renewals and revalidate upon receipt.

TROUBLESHOOTING COMMON ISSUES

- If a subcontractor uses another subcontractor: Require flow-down clauses so that the lower-tier subs carry equivalent insurance, and name the general contractor as additional insured.
- Out-of-state carriers: Accept admitted/non-admitted carriers only if the contract allows; validate carrier ratings where required.
- Subs with no insurance or insufficient limits: Do not allow them on the worksite until they are compliant; for small one-off exposures you might secure a wrap-up or buy-down policy, but include costs in change orders.

CASE EXAMPLES

- A small trade with an expired COI led to uncovered injury claim. The general contractor bore large legal defense costs. The lesson learned: Continuous tracking and enforcement prevent exposure.
- A sub supplied a COI that listed the general contractor as a "certificate holder" but not "additional insured." The case settled for more than the policy limit because the general contractor lacked proper endorsement. The lesson learned: Require endorsements, not just COIs.

RECORDKEEPING AND LEGAL DEFENSE

- Keep copies of every COI, endorsement, and correspondence.
- If litigation arises, records show due diligence in risk management.
- Document any of your enforcement steps taken against noncompliant subs to demonstrate reasonable efforts to manage risk.

IMPLEMENTATION TIPS FOR SMALL- AND MID-SIZE BUILDERS

- Start simple: Create a single standard checklist and require it with every COI.
- If investing in full software isn't feasible, use affordable cloud storage and calendar alerts.
- When your project volume grows beyond your administrative capacity, consider outsourcing to an insurance-savvy third party.
- Train your project managers to spot obvious COI red flags, such as missing endorsements, incorrect names, and expired dates.

CONCLUSION: MAKE INSURANCE COMPLIANCE A CORE PROJECT CONTROL

Insurance is not an administrative afterthought. It's a critical risk transfer mechanism that protects your balance sheet, reputation, and ability to keep building. By setting clear contractual requirements, standardizing submissions, verifying documentation, tracking renewals, and enforcing compliance, builders and general contractors can drastically reduce exposure and focus on delivering quality projects.

AFTERWORD

Partnering with EZCert allows contractors to subcontract the time and effort that goes into documenting insurance compliance. It is a payroll burden reducer. We can help any contractor get their noncompliant subcontractors into compliance, so they can continue growing their business.

Proper insurance coverage reduces the risk of litigation. And of course, litigation usually has a deterrent effect on growth. So, the more we can do to reduce litigation in a business, the better that business can grow and produce results.

This is truly the end result that EZCert brings to the table. We are on the job every day, maintaining the insurance certificates on all the subcontractors, and asking for the revision or the renewal certificates on all the subs.

PROGRAM INSURANCE GROUP

An additional benefit of working with EZCert is our partner, Program Insurance Group. Once we begin working with a company, we are able to set up groups of people for buying opportunities. We deliver a better product price and a better product. By lumping all these brands in the same bucket, we're able to shop that insurance premium at the bigger number based on the number of locations in the system. Overall, we end up with better products, service, and control of the product. And we end up with a better insurance world that way.

Today, smart contractors know that there is somebody watching their insurance. They know that they can come to the Program Insurance Group, purchase insurance coverages for their stores, and access prices lower than those normally offered to them locally.

ABOUT THE AUTHOR

Doug Groves is the force behind Program Insurance Group and its affiliate EZCert Management. Doug has more than 30 years of experience in the insurance industry. With his multifaceted background as an Area Developer for multiple franchises, Doug brings the expertise of the franchise industry to Program Insurance and Certificate Management Services. He maintains ownership in two insurance agencies and continues to do franchise development. He has a wife, three adult children, and is an avid outdoorsman. Doug is passionate about philanthropy and is filled with an entrepreneurial spirit. He can be reached at dgroves@ higginbotham.com.

FOR MORE INFORMATION

Visit EZCert at certmgmt.com or call 844-744-7526.

Visit Program Insurance Group at www.pigbcs.com or also at www.programinsurancegroup.com or call 844-744-7526.

Beyond working with our clients and generating their reports, EZCert also writes articles once a month for the brands about exposures that they have and the coverages that are available for the owners to purchase. We want our clients to know what's going on and what they need to do to protect their businesses.

Our clients are like family. Once we start doing EZCert work, we end up meeting them across the country. We attend their conferences and trade shows.

Together, EZCert and Program Insurance Group stand ready to help your brand grow—both in insurance compliance and in satisfaction with your subcontractors and their insurance programs. Over time, you can lower costs, improve coverage, and reduce the amount of claims for your brand.

EZCert and Program Insurance Group stand ready to help you maintain your insurance compliance throughout the year on all your locations—quickly and seamlessly.